Tiny drops of Kindness

Written by Sally Sun

Illustrated by Maria Riaz

This is Luke, a kind and friendly little guy.

And this is Luke's Yellow Umbrella that keeps him dry.

When it rains, Luke watches for people outside.

He quickly runs out to help keep them dry!

His Yellow Umbrella is big and bright!

It's SO bright it can even be seen at night.

Once Luke was peering outside on a rainy day,

when suddenly he spotted a girl carrying a mound of clay.

But when he looked closer, he realized what she had.

It was her art project...a clay frog on a clay lily pad.

5

Luke knew he had to help right away,

so he grabbed his umbrella and ran out to save the day.

"I can't let my project get wet!" cried the girl in distress.

She was barely covering it with a bit of her dress.

But Luke caught up and shielded her fast.

School →

She made it to school and her project passed!

The next day it rained too, so Luke peered out again,

to see if any wet strangers needed a friend.

10

It was a man on his way to his first job interview,

but the rain was turning his hair gel to goo!

So Luke ran out again to open his umbrella,

blocking the rain for this hardworking fella.

His hair had been saved, and his suit was still dry.

He was going to get the job on his first try!

So the boy gave Luke his phone number to call.

He said, "Call me if YOU ever need anything at all!"

The day after that it rained even more.

Only this time it was a major downpour.

So Luke kept his eyes peeled ready to help any others.

He spotted a young woman with a pie for her mother.

She was holding a pie and trying to be quick,

to hurry to her mother who had been feeling quite sick.

So Luke hurried outside once again to save the day,

to prevent the pie from being washed away.

He sprung open his yellow umbrella and kept her dry.

She was so grateful that Luke had shielded her from the sky!

Luke went back inside and found a good book to read.

He had helped a lot of people and was very pleased.

But little did Luke know,

that there was still more of the story to go.

His kind actions played a major role,

in helping each person achieve their goal!

After the girl got a gold star for her perfect score.

She decided to pursue art even more!

So she sculpted bigger animals and made beautiful pots all day.

And everyone in town wanted to buy her beautiful works of clay!

The man that was interviewing for his first job did well too.

He got the job thanks to Luke saving his hairdo!

He loved his new job and wanted to give back.

So he bought a hungry boy some tasty snacks.

But what about the woman with the pie?

Luke's kindness did so much more than just keep her dry.

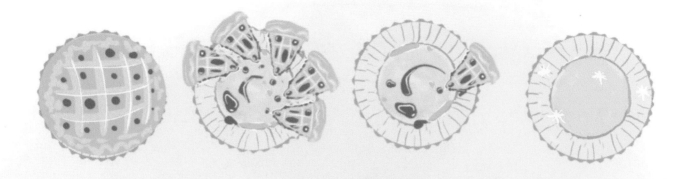

She delivered the pie, and her mother ate every bite.

It was so delicious it made her better overnight!

But then one day Luke's umbrella broke from a heavy wind and rain started filling his boots up to his shins!

He didn't know what to do,

until a familiar voice called out, "Hey you!"

It was the man who got the job! He was riding his bike.

"Hop on!" he said to Luke, "and don't put up a fight!"

So Luke hopped on, and they rode back to Luke's house.

But Luke was all wet, he was totally doused!

But luckily someone else noticed Luke in need.

It was the girl with the art project returning a good deed.

She gave Luke her favorite towel and helped him get dry.

They were both being so kind and helpful, but why?

Then suddenly, Luke knew.

His kindness was coming back to help HIM too!

Once Luke was all dry he noticed a lovely smell.

He found an apple pie at his door after hearing the doorbell.

The young woman baked him the most delicious pie.

But Luke was even more excited to see the new yellow umbrella keeping it dry.

So Luke learned an amazing lesson at the end of the day...

That being kind to others will bring kindness back
YOUR way!

Kindness is spreading sunshine into people's lives regardlesss of the weather.

Printed in Great Britain
by Amazon